the
MUNR

by James Gracie

SEPT NAMES INCLUDE:

Dingwall	**MacCulloch**
Foulis	**Monroe**
Keddie	**Vass**

the MUNROS

MOTTO: Dread God

CREST: A perching eagle

PLANT BADGE: Common Club Moss

TERRITORY: Easter Ross

Tartan featured on the cover is Munro Ancient

Published by Lang Syne Publishers Ltd. Clydeway Centre,
Strathclyde Business Centre, 120 Carstairs Street, Glasgow G40 4DJ
Printed by Thomson Litho, East Kilbride
Design by The Quick Brown Fox Company (Scotland) Limited
© Lang Syne Publishers Ltd. 1997.
ISBN 185 217 080-8
ISBN 978-1-85217-080-6

Reprinted 2007

The Origins
of the
Clan System

by Rennie McOwan

The original Scottish clans of the Highlands and the great families of the Lowlands and Borders were gatherings of families, relatives, allies and neighbours for mutual protection against rivals or invaders.

Scotland experienced invasion from the

Vikings, the Romans and English armies from the south.

The Norman invasion of what is now England also had an influence on land-holding in Scotland. Some of these invaders stayed on and in time became 'Scottish'.

The word clan derives from the Gaelic language term 'clann', meaning children, and it was first used many centuries ago as communities were formed around tribal lands in glens and mountain fastnesses.

The format of clans changed over the centuries, but at its best the chief and his family held the land on behalf of all, like trustees, and the ordinary clansmen and women believed they had a blood relationship with the founder of their clan.

There were two way duties and obligations.

An inadequate chief could be deposed and replaced by someone of greater ability.

Clan people had an immense pride in race.

Their relationship with the chief was like adult children to a father and they had a real dignity.

The concept of clanship is very old and a more feudal notion of authority gradually crept in.

Pictland, for instance, was divided into seven principalities ruled by feudal leaders who were the strongest and most charismatic leaders of their particular groups.

By the 6th century the 'British' kingdoms of Strathclyde, Lothian and Celtic Dalriada (Argyll) had emerged and Scotland, as one nation began to take shape in the time of King Kenneth MacAlpin.

Some chiefs claimed descent from ancient kings which may not have been accurate in every case.

By the 12th and 13th centuries the clans and families were more strongly brought under the central control of Scottish monarchs.

Lands were awarded and administered more and more under royal favour, yet the power of the area clan chiefs was still very great.

The long wars to ensure Scotland's independence against the expansionist ideas of English monarchs extended the influence of some clans and reduced the lands of others.

Those who supported Scotland's greatest king, Robert the Bruce, were awarded the territories of the families who had opposed his claim to the Scottish throne.

In the Scottish Borders country – the notorious Debatable Lands – the great families built up a ferocious reputation for providing warlike men accustomed to raiding into England and occasionally fighting one another.

Chiefs had the power to dispense justice and to confiscate lands and clan warfare produced a society where martial virtues – courage, hardiness, tenacity – were greatly admired.

Gradually the relationship between the clans and the Crown became strained as Scottish monarchs became more orientated to life in the Lowlands and, on occasions, towards England.

The Highland clans spoke a different language, Gaelic, whereas the language of

Lowland Scotland and the court was Scots and in more modern times, English.

Highlands dressed differently, had different customs, and their wild mountain land sometimes seemed almost foreign to people living in the Lowlands.

It must be emphasised that Gaelic culture was very rich and story-telling, poetry, piping, the clarsach (harp) and other music all flourished and were greatly respected.

Highland culture was different from other parts of Scotland but it was not inferior or less sophisticated.

Central Government, whether in Edinburgh or London, sometimes saw the Gaelic clans as a challenge to their authority and some sent expeditions into the Highlands and west to crush the power of the Lords of the Isles.

Nevertheless, when the 18th century Jacobite Risings came along the cause of the Stuarts was mainly supported by Highland clans.

The word Jacobite comes from the Latin for James – Jacobus.

They wanted to restore the exiled Stuarts to the throne of Britain.

The monarchies of Scotland and England became one in 1603 when King James VI of Scotland (1st of England) gained the English throne after Queen Elizabeth died.

The Union of Parliaments of Scotland and England, the Treaty of Union, took place in 1707.

Some Highland clans, of course, and Lowland families opposed the Jacobites and supported the incoming Hanoverians.

After the Jacobite cause finally went down at Culloden in 1746 a kind of ethnic cleansing took place. The power of the chiefs was curtailed.

Tartan and the pipes were banned in law.

Many emigrated, some because they wanted to, some because they were evicted by force.

In addition, many Highlanders left for the cities of the south to seek work.

Many of the clan lands became home to sheep and deer shooting estates.

But the warlike traditions of the clans and

the great Lowland and Border families lived on.

Their descendants fought bravely for freedom in two world wars.

Remember the men from whence you came, says the Gaelic proverb, and to that could be added the role of many heroic women.

The spirit of the clan, of having roots, whether Highland or Lowland, means much to thousands of people.

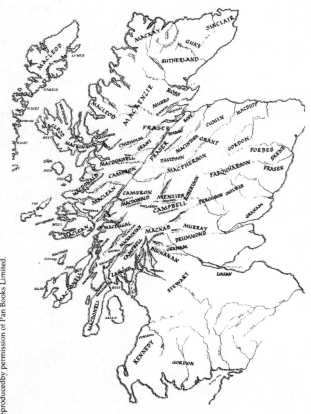

A map of the Clans Homelands.

CHAPTER ONE:
THE MEN OF FERINDONALD

The fighting Munros!

The Munros are thought to be of Celtic origin, and there is a tradition that the name means "man from Roe", Roe being a river in Derry, Ireland.

This "man from Roe" was supposed to have been Donald, son of O'Cathain, who came from Ireland to fight for Malcolm II (1004-34) against the Danes.

The heartland of the clan is a narrow strip of country running eight miles along the northern shore of the Cromarty Firth from Dingwall to Alness.

This was backed by a mountain range which offered protection from attack from the north. To the south was the Cromarty Firth, also easily defended. The western approaches, through Dingwall, were defended by Dingwall Castle, which is now a sparse ruin.

So the early Munros who settled there would have been farmers and fishermen. The soil was fertile, and the shallow Firth was protected from the storms of the open sea. Their main stronghold was Foulis Castle, which eventually became home to the clan chief.

This territory was called Ferindonald (Fearan Domhnuill, "Donald's land"), and was said to be named after this Donald from Ireland. However, the "man from Roe" tradition is now discounted.

Over the years, the name "Munro" has evolved into four main spellings: Munro,

Monro, ÓMunroe and Monroe. In Gaelic, the Munros form Clann an Rothaich.

It is claimed that they held their territory as vassals of the earls of Ross, and that their payment was to present a snowball to the earl every midsummer's day.

Finding snow in summer would not have been difficult. Not far away is Ben Wyvis, and its northern corries usually retain snow all year round.

Queen Elizabeth II is a descendent of these earls of Ross, and could still claim the snowball if she wished.

There were also small pockets of Munros in Tain and further north in Sutherland. Some Munros established themselves south of the Cromarty Firth, on the Black Isle, though this was Mackenzie country. The Munro chiefs were at one time buried there within Fortrose Cathedral.

The first written record we have of a Munro in Ferindonald is of Hugh Munro de Foulis, who died in 1126. He was granted a charter of land by William, Earl of Sutherland.

We find a Robert Munro mentioned in 1309, when Robert 1 granted him lands in Strathspey. And in 1338 George Munro witnessed a charter of lands in Badenoch. Even then, it seems, the Munros were spreading from their heartland.

In 1364 another Robert Munro was granted a charter for more land near Foulis. He is regarded as the first chief of clan Munro.

He married Jane Ross, niece of Queen Euphemia, Robert II's wife. He was "baron baillie" to the earl of Ross, and was killed while defending the earl in this capacity.

There is no record of the Munros fighting in the Wars of Independence with Sir William Wallace. However, William, earl of Ross, was involved, and they may have fought under his name and banner.

This William was captured at the Battle of Dunbar in 1296, and several years in England converted him to Edward I's cause. He took no part in the Battle of Bannockburn, even though he paid homage (unwillingly) to Robert the Bruce in 1308.

William Munro was captured at the Battle of Dunbar in 1296.

His younger brother Sir Walter de Ros did fight at Bannockburn, and was killed there. There is a tradition that a Robert Munro de Foulis fought under William's banner, and that he and his son George were killed as well.

The next earl of Ross was Robert the Bruce's brother-in-law. He fought alongside his King, and was killed at Halidon Hill near Berwick in 1333. Also killed were many of his Munro supporters.

The battle of Halidon Hill.

CHAPTER TWO:
FIGHTING MEN AND MINISTERS

In the early 15th century, James I was held captive by the English. He returned in 1424, and set about consolidating his position.

He harried many Highland houses, such as Strathearn, Mar and the Isles. This was not only to strengthen his position, but to clean up an area rife with feuding. One of the feuds was between the Munros and a branch of the Macdonalds.

Feuding was rife.

Near Strathpeffer, to the west of Dingwall, is the Eagle Stone. This is carved with Pictish symbols, and tradition says it also commemorates a Munro victory over the Macdonalds in 1411.

The Brahan Seer prophesied that if the stone fell over three times, ships could be tethered to it without leaving the sea. It has already fallen over twice, and the stone is now securely held in place.

James signed a document freeing individuals from punishment for past wrong doings.

While harrying some clans, James excused the misdeeds of others. At Inverness in 1428, for instance, he signed a document which freed 28 individuals from punishment for past wrongdoings.

The first five persons are Munros, and no doubt one of the "crimes" was the feud with the Macdonalds. James obviously needed them as allies.

They gained more lands, and began to spread. However, they still continued to bicker with other clans. In 1452 they fought with Mackenzie rebels at Garbat, near Ben Wyvis. The rebels had captured a kinsman of the earl of Ross, and the Munros were trying to release him.

Fighters on both sides tied their shoes to their breasts to deflect arrows, and the location of the skirmish became known as Bealach nam Bròg is now a pipe tune closely associated with the clan.

In 1454, John Munro, tutor of Foulis, forayed south into Perthshire with a band of men to capture cattle. On his way home through Mackintosh country, he disagreed with them as to how many cattle he should give them to allow safe passage.

No agreement was reached, so John Munro and his men headed north with the Mackintoshes in pursuit. At Clachnaharry near Inverness they caught up, and battle commenced. Most Munros made it home, but John Munro himself was maimed for life.

There is no actual record of the Munros fighting at Flodden, but there is a tradition that the Argyllshire Munros are descended from a wounded clan member who survived that battle. We do know, however, that Robert Munro of Foulis was killed at the Battle of Pinkie in 1547.

Robert's son was Robert Mòr ("Great Robert") Munro of Foulis. His first wife's father was a friend of Mary of Guise, Mary Queen of Scots' mother, and because of this Robert himself supported Mary.

His second wife was a much more interesting character. Her name was Katherine, and she was regarded as a witch.

Robert Munro of Foulis was killed at the Battle of Pinkie in 1547.

Katherine and her son stood trial accused of practising witchcraft.

She also introduced Hector, one of her stepsons, to witchcraft, and after Robert's death both stood trial but were acquitted.

In 1617, Robert Dubh Munro of Foulis, 18th clan chief and nicknamed the "Black Baron", became an officer in a regiment that fought for the King of Denmark against the Catholics.

This force was entirely made up of Highland Protestants, with Robert Dubh's company comprising 700 men, all Munros.

Eventually the regiment fought in Sweden, and many Munros switched from this regiment to the Swedish army proper, where they rose to high rank.

Robert Dubh died in 1633, and his brother Hector succeeded him. In 1634, while in London, he was received by Charles I, who made him a Baronet of Nova Scotia.

Most of the Munros were Presbyterians, though a fair number embraced Episcopalianism. Some, however, never forsook the Roman Catholic religion of their ancestors.

Robert Munro, a priest of the Roman Catholic church, died while a prisoner in Invergarry Castle in 1704 after a lifetime of clandestine missionary work in Scotland.

There are, in France, a number of Munro families who claim descent from one Ulysses Monroe, who was a cavalier during the English Civil War.

And after the Battle of Worcester in 1651, several Munros fighting on the Royalist side were deported to North America. Many American Munros claim descent from these deportees.

In fact, the first person to fire a shot in the American War of Independence was William Munroe, at Lexington in 1775. It is also recorded that sixteen Munros took part in the Lexington battle.

The Rev. Alexander Monro, Principal of Edinburgh University, left Scotland in 1691 rather than belong to a church which didn't recognise bishops. His grandson John was with the Jacobite court in Rome in 1746.

Sir Robert Munro, who became clan chief

in 1729, joined the Black Watch regiment of the Hanovarian Army in 1740, and eventually became the colonel of an English regiment, the 37th Foot.

His son Harry joined the Earl of Loudoun's regiment, and both fought against Bonnie Prince Charlie. Two hundred Munro volunteers joined them.

Harry was captured at Prestonpans in 1745, and Robert and his brother Duncan were killed at Falkirk in 1746.

When the Jacobite Uprising had been suppressed, Sir Harry did his best to see that Jacobite prisoners were treated humanely.

He and his clan had suffered under the Jacobites, but he made no claim for compensation. However, some money did come his way, and the mighty Earl of Sutherland proclaimed that the "little tribe of Munros" had been given too much.

The Battle of Prestonpans where Harry Munro was captured.

CHAPTER THREE:
A SETTLED EXISTENCE

In 1750, Sir Harry had Foulis Castle rebuilt to reflect his status as 7th baronet, clan chief and member of parliament. Since then, the clan has led a more settled existence.

There have been many famous members, some distinguishing themselves through service to their country, some through service to their country, some through literature, and some in sporting fields.

The 11th baronet, Sir Hector Munro, commanded the 3rd Battalion of the Seaforth Highlanders during the Boer War of 1899-1903. He was also lord lieutenant of Ross and Cromarty. His younger son Hector was killed during the last days of the First World War.

As the older son had died in infancy, this meant that there was no direct heir. The baronetcy moved from the Foulis branch of the family to that of Foulis-Obsdale.

One of the most famous Munros was Neil

(1864-1930), a journalist who wrote the Para Handy tales. Even though he came from the Argyll branch of the family, he used the pen name "Hugh Foulis".

Another famous Munro – but spelling his name differently – was James Monroe (1758-1831), 5th president of the United States. He was descended from a Royalist Munro who had been deported to America after fighting at the Battle of Preston in 1648.

It was James Monroe who formulated the famous "Monroe Doctrine", which set out the

A scene from the television version of Para Handy tales, created by Neil Munro.

American continent's relationship with European colonial powers.

The city of Monrovia, capital of Liberia, is named after him.

Sir Hugh Thomas Munro (1856-1919) was a Scot born in London. He was a famous mountaineer, and all mountains in Scotland over 3,000 ft are now called "Munros".

Sir Hugh himself never managed to climb them all, but "Munro bagging" has become a popular sport.

These then are the Munros. It is a recorded fact that no Munro ever emigrated because of the actions of his chief, and that no Munro was ever evicted to allow sheep onto his land.

But the Munros have still managed to spread across the world, from Canada to New Zealand, and you meet the name wherever Scots men and women have settled.

Munros travelled the seas of the world to settle in new lands as far apart as Canada and
New Zealand.

A Settled Existence

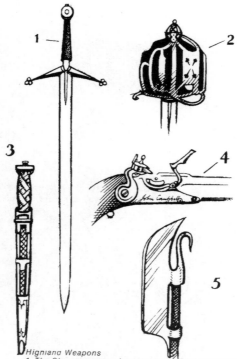

Highland Weapons
1. The Claymore or two-handed sword (Fifteenth or early Sixteenth century)
2. Basket hilt of Broadsword made in Stirling, 1716
3. Highland Dirk — Eighteenth century
4. Steel Pistol (detail) made in Doune
5. Head of Lochaber Axe as carried in the 45 and earlier.